AF613991

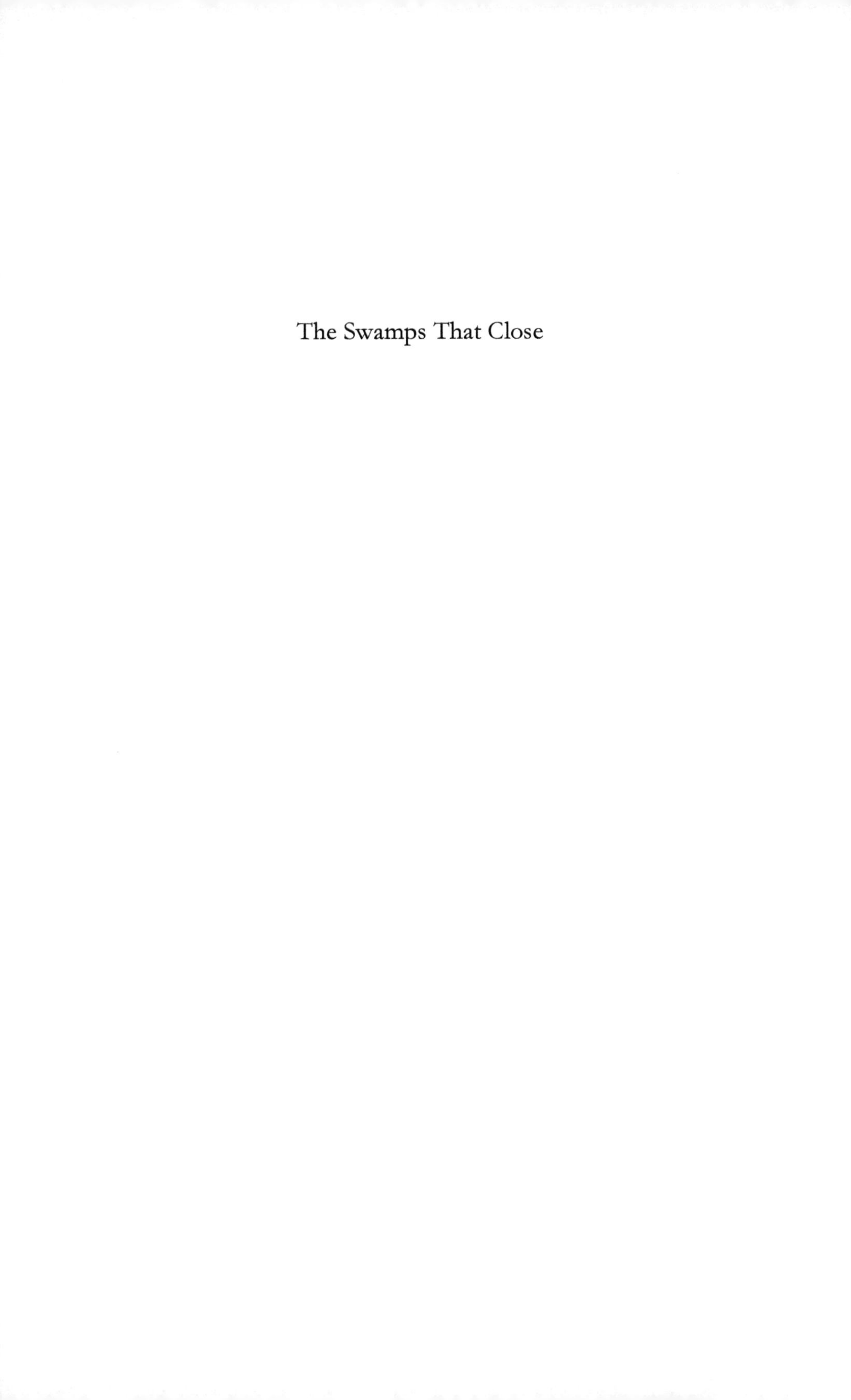

The Swamps That Close

The Swamps That Close

Tyler Johnson

www.lulu.com/tyler

The Swamps That Close
© 2004 by Tyler Johnson
ISBN 1 4116 1267 1

Poetry

10 9 8 7 6 5 4 3 2

All rights reserved. No part of this publication may be reproduced, stored in a retrieval system, or transmitted in any form or by any means, electronic, mechanical, photocopying, recording or otherwise, without the prior permission of the publishers and/or authors.

'The Boat Builders' originally appeared in The Carolina Quarterly, Volume 45.1, 1992 at the University of North Carolina, Chapel Hill, NC 27599

Published through lulu.com, http://www.lulu.com/tyler

Contents

Just For The Fun Of It

A Crush Of Poems

Getting In Touch With The Frequencies

Acknowledgements

for Irving, Rodney, Scott, those that followed
and the paths you've set us on.

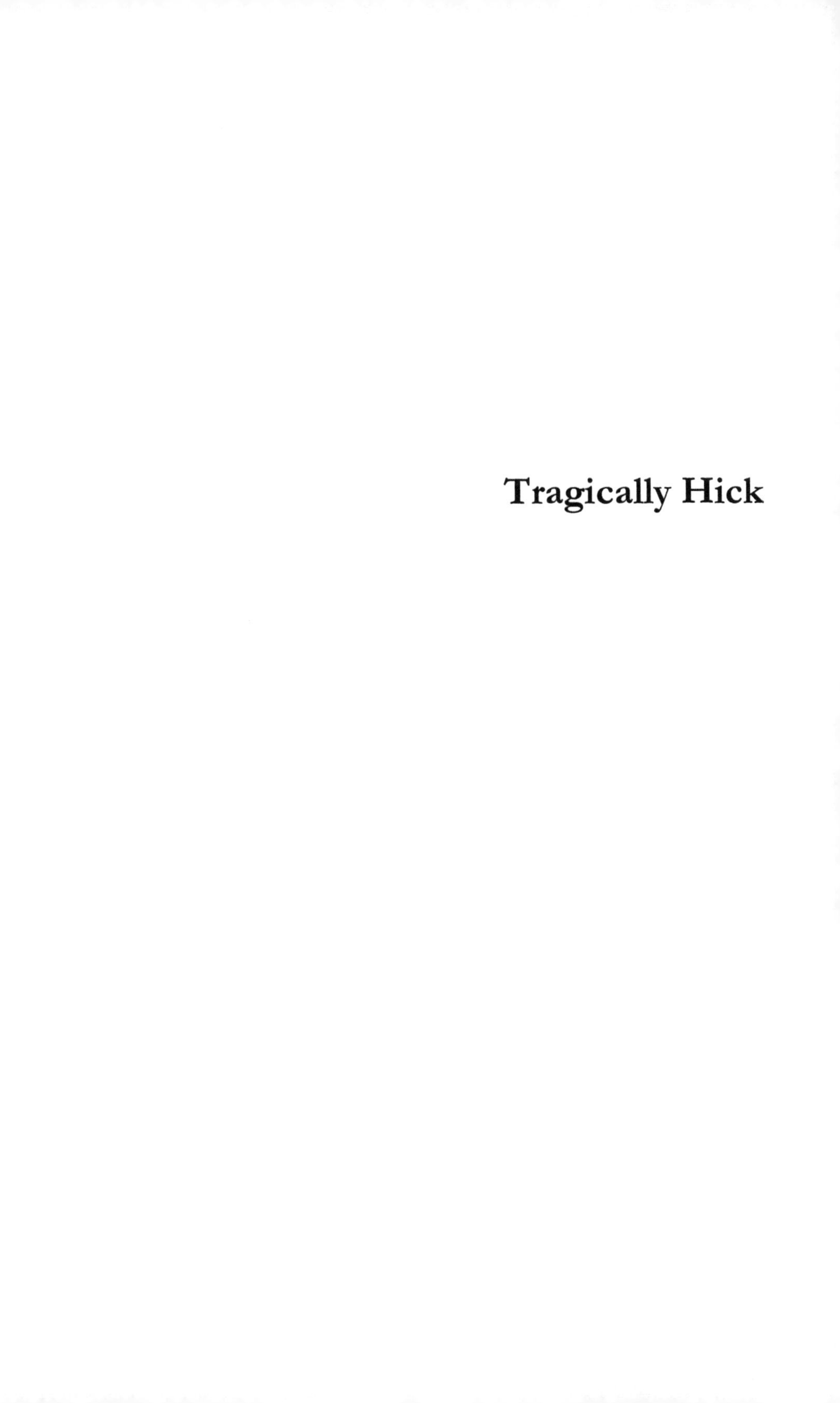

Tragically Hick

Gram Rides In Back

Jesus in rock
the only warm spot on the dial
glowing in the cab of an old black Ford,
they roll through kneaded green hills,
past towel outlets and stands
of hot boiled peanuts.
In the back of the truck
Gram fumbles for Mary Janes
to share with the dog,
one hand holding the yellow cap,
his red eyes watching
the creosote fence, fields of clay
vanish up and down
behind them.

Near Hamilton he will crawl
from the bed of the truck,
ease gray work boots onto the gravel
and walk the mile home,
his friends rolling on past Helltown.
It is this mile that lays him down,
these acres of broom straw and field corn,
stopping to breathe
and lumber down the path
where crickets rock
him gently
asleep.

Hog Killing

We sat in jeans and boots on the fence,
nursing bottles of Wild Turkey,
betting on the tall one or ...
the one with fat sides.
Aim is a hard thing to take.
At four feet, you couldn't use the scope,
and a .22 hollow point needed to hit a pig
right between the eyes.

The rifle clapped in the forehead.
Her sisters fought for a place beneath her head
to lap the wild blood,
and drove her
crying, around the pen.
We shot her in four different corners
and once on the ground
before she finally shut up.
Beating the pigs away, we roped her
but couldn't pull her out
without a truck.

There was a block and tackle hung
from a salt treated two by six stand.
This morning's fire was already making steam
pour from the mouth of our fifty–five gallon drum.
Bled, and spiked through the Achilles tendon,
we lowered her headfirst into the scald.

Still wet, we nailed her feet to our table
and tore away her red hair
with paint scrapers.
The heavy blade of a Buck
cut tough fat in a line
from throat to crotch.
I put my hand inside her, holding,
until we slid the bucket to our table
and let go, filling it with steamy entrails.
We gave her warm, swollen bladder to the dogs
as a joke.
Hosing the flattened carcass,
slick, white ribs nestled in bacon,
we cut away hock,
tore hunks of her cheek
for sausage.

Moly West

Forty–three years with the State Highway Department
crawling that big yellow truck over
every road west
of the South Anna River.
Together they'd nosed through ditches
and broken lines,
found Hanover's favorite beer bottle,
mailbox, hubcap,
and possum fatality.
He knew us by our yards
or driveways,
or the corn we kept,
and each night saw
whose tractor slept outside
on the way to park his truck
in its own gravel bed.

The stubby patch of hair
on his pink head
was wry, just awakened,
but perfect for scratching...
and thinking.
He was strange because
he'd never been to school,
and he mumbled so badly
I could hardly make out what he said,
But I'd agree!

Agree that my five and his sixty–seven
were just too much
for one afternoon.

In his house was a deer's head
hung high on the wall
with glassy eyes so full of questions
that I made them cover it up
with a coat,
and sat in the kitchen
watching Mabel can
or preserve.

Out back the hounds bay
starved, but fast,
and the coons knew
whose garden they robbed.
Moly remembered
when our fire tower was built,
like a steel scarecrow,
hands on hips,
the highest thing in our county.
It was one small step,
almost unbelieving.
Had we ever really
been to the moon?

Self Serve Island

it's a boy's walk between the tracks
and a main drag
white washed brick of
one time gas emporium now
a mall for the under classed

the cabinet shop where
Mr. Mann fits a toy wooden arm
to toddler rocker
says he needs to "stain" it
I hope not too much

Tattoo Parlor offers
needled Ace of Spades for you
or a friend's arm.
photos of green art
on muscle, tit, thigh,
tacked on the cork wall like
pictures of prize bass
(touch the '58 Caddy in the lot–
Lord knows what you might
get stuck with)

RAY'S ELECTRICAL
"can rebuild starters, alternators, ..."
but not put hair or teeth
back in his head.

Unending power,
his battery sale may outlast
the sun.

Tenneco the place to go
for Twinkies, toilet paper,
Harley– Davidson jewelry,
girls in jean shorts playing Pacman
and not afraid of being eaten.
it's a boy's walk
in the light from Self Serve Island
traps him on the
street sign says

ig rettes snack BQ
Jimcup REG 1.02

Lake Lanier

No longer able to frisbee
we lie hog– happy
on beach towels
fallen like cards
on the sloping green
lawn.

A small boy is clutching
at the shore
a life– sized inflatable
Pink Panther.
The red and white buoys wag
in the green water
like sixteen ounce beer cans
advertising "DANGER" and "KEEP OUT".

Tonight
we will close the cooler,
fling towels and shoes
into the car,
let the cool air blow us back
down winding roads,
through deer crossings,
toward the darkness of Atlanta.
Through the dark
to the lighted dance floors,
the midway of Memorial Drive.

Back

to our home beside the highway

where we sleep

to the gentle rush of traffic

breaking like waves

across the median.

Walking

I have walked a thousand miles
pounding out my troubles, wonders
on the pavement, working out my mind
like a stiff muscle. We share this
walking therapy.

By 1941 you had covered most of Richmond,
World War II, and ways to face technology.
In 1987 I did Atlanta, what to do
with technology, and took a stab
at literature.
In a few generations we will know everything
or we will have walked ourselves
into the earth like the spreading of seeds
or families.

The fascinated hours I've spent in hardware stores
are a repeat of your youth.
When I light my pipe I take your pleasure.
The way I watch girls is ours.
Projects: my mandolin, your wooden ship,
our rotten luck at fishing.
You tinker in woods and metals,
I, in music and words.

We share the art of being awe– struck

by the nature of Things.

When you die, I die.

When I live, you must live.

How, how,

how

can a man love so much,

a boy reach so far ?

Christmas Telescope

We crossed the road into the city cemetery
to look at the sun.

There are no tombstones.
Only copper plates on a mown field
and two monuments of Christ
to honor a city's dead.

The sun was green
above my father's telescope.
The gray hill reflected roundly
in the chrome legs
of his new tripod.

We capped the scope.
At the road I remember
watching car of car
of old man pass,
grinning creature smile
with growing nose and balding neck,
huge ears, his own Christmas hat.

The Smithy

Tiny red bullets fly
at the chisel's touch.
Each strike of his hammer tolls another angle
of the church he carves into his shield.
White hot, the flat iron is beaten into tower,
full bricked steeple, and cools to icy black.
The clutter of plates leans on every crevice,
hammered lamps, the petrified faces
pounded back into life on flasks and goblets.
Miniature crosses scatter on the sill
in the distorted light from leaden glass.
Rain drips onto iron pots
hung from the shop front beam,
his advertisement, kettles to end up
planters in modern German yards.

The street is racked with plastic souvenirs,
trinkets to market without barter,
all bearing the half– tower motif
of the church destroyed in the war.
Above the town, fog, hearing no bell or recoil,
drifts from gullies, in the highest spruces
like smoke from restless cannons,
leaves the sound of tires on cobblestone,
rain washing terra cotta roofs,
cataracts of oil
pouring through bricked streets.

I– 85 Cloverleaf

Under Construction

Each day it grows,
inching, sliding forward,
dragging the bulk of broken rock,
pushing ahead the rubble,
a structure that pops like bones.
Raucous cranes dip and bow,
seeing far down the gouge
to its smooth tail:
the honeycomb– sided highway.

Each night those cranes sleep wary, erect,
fearing a deadly ping
beneath this creeping glacier
that is newer than I
or the slowly lapping mud.

Uncovering A Dinosaur

with thanks to the Georgia Department of Transportation

Early mornings we passed
the first diggings,
evidence of a tail,
spiny vertebrae
running several yards and
plunging into the Dunwoody soil.
They must have known
it was going to be a big one.
Archaeologists commanded hard hats,
pulled out the portable, flashing arrows,
calculated and began to draw
her broad body.
Graphwork in timber, steel,
bones wired in place,
they unearthed the back and
ribs and
the neck.
Pylons roped off the crowds
in a sort of drive–in museum
of natural history.
She roared and stamped
at I– 85
running south between her legs,
and held still
while we examined her teeth

and belly;
bulldozers, tiny trucks,
cement splattered generators,
the wreckage of things
eaten long ago.

The Swamps That Close

I.

Out of my car,
flat useless tires,
I walk route 671
growing dark.
crickets
bleed
from every
tree
frog throbs from stump
all muscle

the road
softens,
breaks,
painted
white lines
lost
in weedy
asphalt,
my ankles rimmed
in cold, green
water.

low marsh sleeps
with caw
caws and
hoots,
bobbing cattails
rocked
by hunting mice

the breeze is thick, low
flips the green
underleaves
of giant fern,
herds purple
blood cell
clouds.
splash
and groan
of old reptile
rolls from below
shallow swamp.

II.

Out from the house
water bubbles through fields,
roots slither close to touch
warm brick.

The yard cannot restrain the edge of woods.

Jeered by dwarfish underbrush,
wooden fingers grapple
the frightened dogwood.
Planted, she can't hold back
the smooth green buds
urging her skin,
the wild flush
blooming.

The Paths You've Set Us On

The Boat Builders

We build boats in David's garage
because we like the way they feel
when you let them go.
We remember the light
on in the kitchen for so many nights.
How peculiar the whine of a saw
and the skid of lumber on concrete
must be to a neighbor at two in the morning.
We wanted to give them something to find.
Something scattered on beaches like bottles
or birds fresh from death in the morning tide,
something caught in the vines, half sunk,
empty and hollow, something still
alive.

Camouflaged with splotches of moonlight
and shadows from leaves,
we drag the boat, like a body,
toward the baby poplars leaning over the water.
The smell of wet honeysuckle and mud
rotting on the bank
makes me breathe deep
and feel the pulse of frogs
beat in my eyes and throat.

Tonight it is my turn
to wade out with the boat.

Water pulls heavy on blue jeans,
smacks at my chest.
Up to my shoulders, I sway
like something not quite rooted.

From here the sky is deepest,
drowned
in mist and water.
The boat I push I allow
to glide quietly out of reach,
out of slow, running distance,
out of shout.
It may disappear
before I reach the shore,
or may linger
listening to the fog and moon
long after I'm gone,
driven home in silence,
leaning against the window
cold
and trembling
and wet.

Playing Dumb

At dinner your
blouse hung
in purple folds
draped from your
wrist on the
white tablecloth
where you fingered
a silver spoon
on a porcelain saucer.
Frozen
by your
silk cupped breast
I contemplate
the fish belly
softness
beneath your chin.
When you pulled
your hair
from along your
jaw and
tucked it behind
your ear
and turned to me
and smiled you
thought my vacancy
was love.
I have no choice

but to touch my
forehead
and joke the first
news
in my mind.
But it was Nicaragua
not South Africa
you remind me
and think my absence
is cute.
You didn't notice
how precisely
the next couple
laughed off
the same joke they
laughed off
in Alberta.
When the waiter
presented
his tray
you didn't see the
knife in his belt.
You weren't looking
when the holes
in the wall opened
and machine gunned
me down.
You kept

eating as they screamed
and I lay
toppled in my chair,
our faces bursting
in fire
as you took my hand
and we bent
to kiss.
When you speak
I am sorry.
This is suicide.
You think flowers
are still.

A Man Is A Large Animal To Find

A man is a large animal to find,
toppled or heaped,
gathering
brittle leaves.
They are not suited for dragging:
a bent log
through brush or snow.
Frozen arms
cradle a perfect crouch;
the sacred hollow
of his mouth.
When he fell
there was the sound
of a saddle
dropped
and an easy roll.

The Day Comes When I

The day comes when I, beast, stumble in the heat,
feeling my staggering weight swoon
to the dizzy, spinning, uphill fall.
I fight my eyes open, swallow the wretch,
and panting, cannot hold back
the sadness of seeing my world pitch.

What I want is that you would hold my head
and pull back my hair with your fingers
so the sweat will cool my fever,
and whisper so soft, and slow, and low,
to soothe the motion of awakeness,
that I might stomach this sudden surge of life.

Like Rest

Is there a reason
why he finds himself
for the third morning in a row
at the window
trying to rise
with the sun ?

There is no sleep
he discovered
and the night is not so dark
as it is quiet.

Morning will fall again.
Slats of light
will crawl down his face
like rest.

Sydnic

Sydnic had to get more,
he just knew it;
more wide, more water, more home ...
something like that.
There are certain itches
that just grab you by the seat of the pants
and walk you right over a cliff.
Sydnic had to get it,
and soon was as good as anytime.
It was like opening a door.
He would fly off
at the drop of a hat.
You'd think he would've gotten discouraged,
but ...
he wanted to feel the bottom dropping out.
Now he was waiting ...
always that shallow, nervous, breathing,
approaching the well
even to the very edge.

And Not Speak

Only the desperate work the back stairs.

The bereaved, sons whose fathers have died,
the cadets weakly dressed in their space–age tweeds,

a girl, new to womanhood, not knowing what to do
with the five young men she just escorted out the door,

the sick, the lanky, the awkwardly framed,
the man whose head is on fire,
the lame professor, the raging queen

duck the hallways for a chance to breathe easy.
Now eye– shy, it is a place
to hold down the railing, and not speak
of nothing that is wrong.

Each Morning You Start To Wrap

Each morning you start to wrap,
slap my still face with cold whispers and rhymes,
a quieter time as you wind me up.
Pulling the strings that will start the top spinning,
you're good at the twist,
it's all in the wrist as I spin
into the man you've come to love.

At night I tilt homeward
before I run out.
You open the door on my pitiful posture,
I wobble and lean,
put my hand on your shoulder.
I've come unwound before your eyes,
fallen to the floor.
Could I stand I would
tell you how much I love you
and apologize for not being here.
Thank you, Dear,
for dragging me off into bed.

Van Gogh Park, Auvers– sur– Oise

Birds sing across the stone walls
that encircle the park
we built for you.
The rumble of the train reaches
up from the ground
and leaves you –
          track
                    track
                              track
out of town.
At your bronze feet
tourists aim to take your stare
home in their cameras.

How can you stand so straight up
with the weight
of easel
and canvass
strapped
to your back?

Just For The Fun Of It

Settling In

Cow don't poke your curious nose
at me, long neck hanging
over some invisible bucket.
I'll coil and spit into your stupid face,
panic you and your herd,
watch you relocate for hours
forgetting about me.

I, Snake, claim this sun–tilted hill
to sprawl.
Stretch and let the cropped field grass
scratch my back
and stomach
down to my bright, wet (sleek, yeah!) baby skin.
High on eggs, I might just lie
until I rub away.

The Buddy System

WELCOME TO FIRST NATIONAL'S BUDDY SYSTEM.

(flash)

INSERT CARD FOR SERVICE.

‘Instant Access’ (tm) is what we're all about.

Now no more waiting.

Now % No w % No w % No w %

Now % no more errors in your statement.

That fur coat.

That diamond ring.

Cashmere everything.

We're ‘Buy Beautiful’ (tm).

Your Buddy System,

It's only a button away

(the end of the world)

and when we go down

we go down together.

Kellogg's Corn Pops

or Yellow Is Our Color

Kellogg's Corn Pops
Kellogg's Corn Pops
Kellogg's Corn Pops
Kellogg's Corn Pops
Kellogg's Corn Pops explode
in geysers from my bowl,
an old faithful start
to an old faithful day.
Kellogg's Kids kick soccer balls
in my yard.

In a laboratory in Iowa
a bald man
takes a kernel between his fingers,
inflates it with a swizzle,
and dips it in the paint.
Boxcars of Yellow leave Iowa
every morning at seven.

Kellogg's Corn Pops

The Librarian's Dream

The overhead projectors
have taken the school.
They patrol the halls
with siren mirrors.
Books re–shelve themselves.
The typewriter spurts
news of the revolution.
The stereo sets and resets
playing music of the new generation.
Even the televisions
raise their butterfly antennae
ready for takeoff.

An Insult

In your dreams
you are king of all that you see.
Concerned with upholding
your pillow–propped head,
fed your special ambrosia,
you laugh
and wipe the drool
from your pretty chin,
while maidens bathe
your complacent fancy.

Do not complain now,
Royal Flounder,
one eye to the ground,
a sensitive, fleshy creature.

You wheel about like a fat duck
stumbling toward visions of bread.

Sitting Outside The College

Sitting, (comma) outside, (comma)
the college.. (period period)
of law; (semicolon)
eating, sandwiches,
Harley, U.S. Army, duffel bag,
Sunday,
racquetball in the parking lot,
stray kid stalk the newsstand
, Mama never told me there'd be
this many kinds of free.

A Crush Of Poems

The Rail Girl

Collecting wood for twelve years
hasn't made her callous
or smart.
It's just made more tears
in her dress to heal.
From her expectations
she can offer up
rails and fencepost
as a dowry,
skeletal wood
for her chest.

Breathing Through A Straw

(The Asthma Song)

In your chest you carry
– slowly even steps –
a pair of birds
They start!
Flutter and Crash
fly hard against the cage
beat, beat to rise
to fly or lift or
breathe or fall
they fight
they chew
mash the cage between
their beaks and squeeze
and strain with birdlike strength
the isometric bars
they pant
from bony nostrils.

spent,
they flop,
beached,
and fan
trembling wings;
sweaty, downy, gills.

The Lump

for Katie

It may take years,
me not hearing from you,
until I'm
moving through
the back of your head,
talking quietly at your neck.
Just behind your throat
I'll grow old
and not speak at all.

Too Often We Judge A Poem

Too often we judge
a poem
by its production
instead of how it sounds
or feels
when we crush it in our mouths.
I used to

write poems in primer
on the sides of boxcars
that lumbered toward Pittsburgh
and then stole away because
that
was art.

I used to build poems
from stone and packing and glue
but that, too,
lost its market.

Several directions lay open:
oral photographs,
poems made of paper,
and dancing.

The Bow

The violin bow was held
on the wall with tacks,
one to an end,
and the small wooden back,
a tall woman's calf,
held a string of thin tendons
hid behind an elderly shin.

OverPass

In the orange booths of a diner
a man is drinking
more coffee than he needs
to drive.

He peels
the thin paper from a slice of butter
and cuts
half away.

The telephone hangs
beside the glass case
holding apples.

Crossing A Cornfield

Stuffed with hay
to stand up straight,
a little lean
to keep myself forward is

Giant me, ravaging
the corn stubble,
striding waves
of curled red clay –
crested, never breaking.

Blackbirds bark
this winter man
and run, cackling wildly,

"Leave him far behind, below
crossing row and row.
Ha! Leave him far to go !"

Getting In Touch With The Frequencies

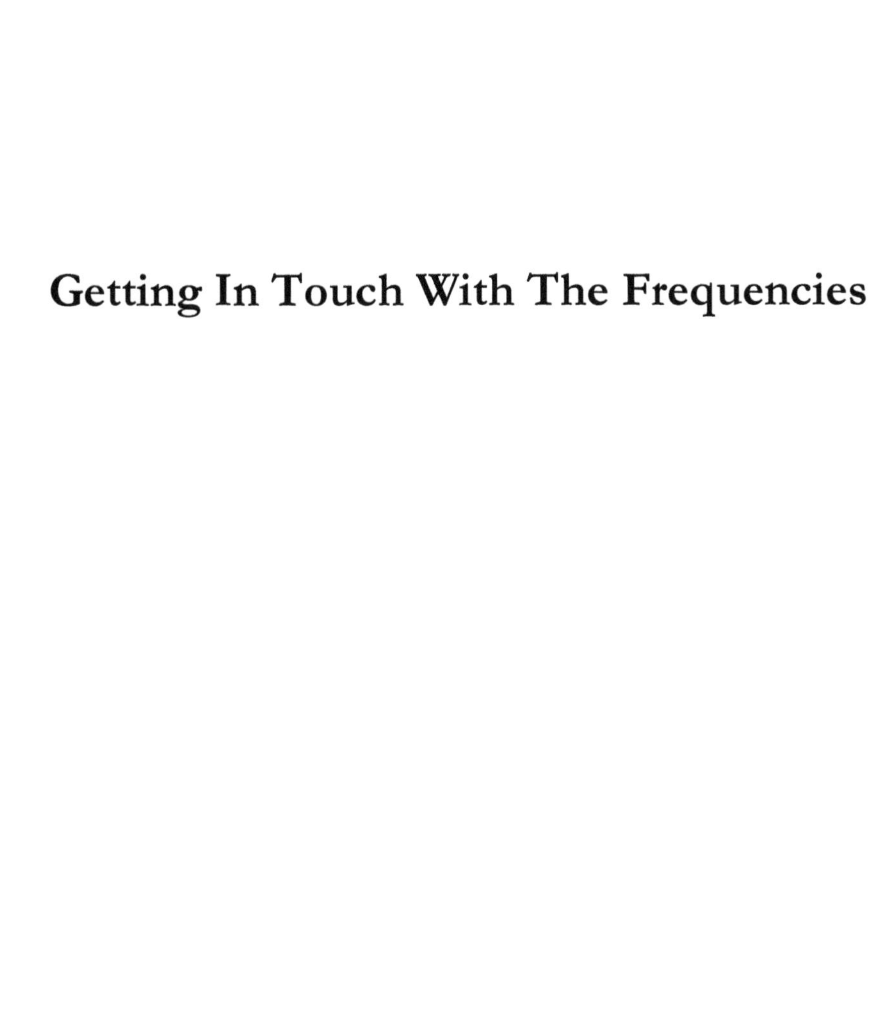

Evo – lution

Your fathers before you
drug their knuckles 'til they could stand,
lived in caves, died slaves,
pinned their foreheads back,
wrote pages in the dirt
so they could learn
what not to be afraid of
in the sky.

You animal
You drip with desire,
stare in the fire,
touch sharp edges
(curious forms in the hedges
for one of a pattern
that started a million years ago),
coat hangers and bathroom walls,
a pearl between the fingers,
timber, steel bridges, bones wired in place,
faces in history books
and looks you learned younger
on friends in an eye opening way.

New Jungle

In the soft plastic corners
of this silent machine
information pours from bus to bus,
trafficked in silicon, channeled
with inaudible purpose, dimensioned,
arrayed, matrixed,
branching,
a function of time,
cyclic.

The throb of your
heart, the beat of your
sex, measures of the earth and moon,
days of the sun,
the loping rhythm of your four–legged run,
ritual melodies on wooden drums

listen ...

New jungle, new fears.

The pad padding pad pad of gang feet
on the sunbeat, black,
macadam cracked streets like
skin on the back of an earlier beast
from some Africa.

We drive an iron horse.
Whipping machines pounding
steel hooves on the desert.
Crank and squeal, they
sweat hot kerosene.
Racked, biting air,
we leave them to burn
or canker across the sand.
They will kick the dust,
snort, when
they are no more
but ribbed chassis, struts,
corroded framework,
callous,
supple,
rust.

I Can Almost Remember

I can almost remember
learning to speak,
pressing my thoughts into soft clay.
Nights like this my jaw grows heavy.
With a thick tongue I taste
the green juice of mashed leaves,
hiding quietly with the beat of my heart.
I know there is something stalking...

Frustration.
Squeeze and mold,
it's like breaking rocks,
cracking nuts.
I can almost remember
drawing on the wall at Lasceaux,
licking my lips like the green snake
sliding through trees.
There is something stalking...

Exhausted.
Lain on the beach,
the muddy inch
where water touches bank,
licking smooth the slime
of our drag from the ocean.

The Maniac's Phone Party

Picking up the phonebook I think
of the contacts at my fingertips,
how right now I could just
buzz the Governor
to chat interchange progress
or talk to the guy in work clothes
and no teeth who sweeps
the parking lot at work.

A thousand delicate pages,
a bible,
a testament
to our numbers' strength.
How the height of our names
raises children
to our tables.
How the weight of them is enough
to keep even paper
from blowing away.

Searching for my own
I find name after name rising
above my fingertip,
each with his or her number,
street, hometown...
memorial to a war
of communication.

Phonebooks and phones
only seconds away
in hospitals, homes, garages,
it is remarkable how closely we hold
the dead.

From breath to transducer our voices,
Synapsed,
less impulse,
than the noise of intelligence.
Our thoughts lifted
to satellite orbit
and shifted any number of degrees
(st
ill thereis distortion   – you can't
see what i mean)

A single message comes down
toward a frog's egg nest
matrix of bubbles,
each with a tiny black spot,
a receiver,
a cord.

Once, Every Endless Time Collapsing, Our Systems Stop and Go

one pulse
The explosion of the universe began a cycle
so vast in period its motion can be described
as a steady–state force.
Infrared, microwave, gamma radiation,
Terra–cycles all the way to DC.

The earth spins
dragging water and wind,
counting our days,
pulling our sex,
breaths, lives.
Low frequency ears,
High frequency eyes,
our feet feel the motion,
the range of vibration,
so sound, so light
we are nothing
but music.

Sexual rhythms
in, out, with the heart
the music we make
feels good
can take us back,
get us in touch
with the frequencies.

Acknowledgements

Thanks to:

The Carolina Quarterly for permission to re–publish 'The Boat Builders' which appeared in volume 45.1. http://www.unc.edu/depts/cqonline/

Gary Sange at Virginia Commonwealth University. Gary showed me the depth to which poems can be a sensory experience.

David Bottoms at Georgia State University and Nikki Giovanni at Virginia Tech for inspiration. Not often mentioned in the same breath, nevertheless providing models for vision, voice, and courage.

The whippoorwill at the log cabin who sang from the cedar tree into my childhood bedroom window every single night. What coded dreams did you sing into my ear?

www.ingramcontent.com/pod-product-compliance
Ingram Content Group UK Ltd.
Pitfield, Milton Keynes, MK11 3LW, UK
UKHW040558210726
13854UKWH00008B/1388

9 781411 612679